What Our Readers Have Said...

Applicability

"These books are great tools that should be used as guidelines for our everyday supervisory practices. You need to take the time to do a short self-evaluation when reading them."

•

"The Pinpoint Training Series delivers information that could be used in a lot different areas."

•

"The things and problems we deal with everyday are discussed in these books."

Convenience

"I like this because I can take them with me to read at a convenient time. I feel the little time I have to spend in the office is best use on activities that directly relate to revenue opportunities. I like the short amount of time it takes to keep up with these."

•

"I prefer the self-study approach; it fits in with my schedule."

•

"I like the fact that the format allows the books to be reviewed as time permits. All work has been conducted on personal, evening/weekend time."

•

"Easy to use... if you put the time into it."

Challenge

"My thought is that the real value of these books comes into effect when doing the action plans."

•

"I like the fact that the format allows assignments to be reviewed as time permits."

Clarity

"Short and sweet. These books are easy to comprehend."

•

"Easy to use, understand, and reference if needed."

Relevance

"I have enjoyed reading these books. They are relevant to today's work environment and the ongoing change in the way we manage our workforce."

•

"I believe the contents of the Pinpoint series are excellent. It causes one to reflect on the daily dynamics in working with oneself as well as with management and peers."

Leadership Styles

Pinpoint Leadership Skill Development Training Series

TIMOTHY F. BEDNARZ

MAJORIUM
BUSINESS PRESS

Pinpoint Leadership Skill Development Training Series
"Leadership Styles"
Timothy F. Bednarz

Graphic design: Monika Pawlak

Majorium Business Press
2025 Main Street
Stevens Point, WI 54481
715.342.1018 • 800.654.4935

ISBN 978-1-62101-045-6

Printed in the United States of America

Introduction

The Pinpoint Leadership Skill Development Training Series is designed for targeted training and education regarding increased improvement in a specific skill or competency.

Each book within this series is designed to be easy to use, understand and apply to your job. It can be used as a basis for training individuals, as a discussion guide or as a personal training tool.

Each chapter within this book discusses a specific concept. When you have completed all eight chapters you should have a 360° perspective of the topic.

Additionally, each chapter is divided into specific sections:

- The first section provides you with an overview of the topic
- The Implications section discusses why the concept is important, and why it is important to learn and apply.
- The Strategies, Tips & Techniques to Apply section teaches how to use and apply the particular concept to your work.
- The Points to Ponder section gives you something to think about or to be discussed with a group setting. These are questions not meant to be immediately answered, but to be pondered over time.
- The Training Activity section provides you with the tools to transfer what you have learned to your job. It is designed to help create an action plan to effectively apply the concept.

Each of the topics in this series is time-tested and proven in the marketplace. They have been used by thousands of employees as training tools. Many of the users have commented that what made these books valuable, was the ability to refer to them when a problem surfaced. They indicated that they remembered reading about the exact problem. They referred back to these books and found an appropriate solution.

You will find them equally valuable as a resource in your professional development library.

Table of Contents

LEARNING OBJECTIVES:

- To identify the critical factors and benefits of leadership styles and their impact.
- To understand the implications and ramifications that enhances or diminishes various leadership styles.
- How to overcome the problems and pitfalls associated with applying specific leadership styles.
- How to apply effective strategies to enhance and develop one's personal leadership style.
- How leadership styles impact the decision making process.

What Leadership Style Is the Real You?

hat makes an effective leader? Each one is defined and known by their unique leadership style. Their style determines how they manage and apply their skills when detailing strategies, motivating employees toward a vision and mission, and developing specific goals that subsequently become financial, organizational and social objectives. Leaders define themselves with their values, personality, communication style and a host of other factors. All of these elements combine into a leadership style that is seen by everyone in the leader's workplace.

IMPLICATIONS — WHAT THIS MEANS TO YOU

Most individuals feel that a leader fits a stereotypical mold. When asked to define a leader, individuals might cite Colin Powell, Ronald Reagan, Jack Welch or Bill Gates. Yet each of these people developed a unique, individual leadership style. While all leaders have specific characteristics in common, the way they apply their style to communicate passion, direction and information is as unique as their own set of personal characteristics.

It is important for leaders to understand that they must be true to themselves. Effective leaders don't mimic another's style. If they did, it would come across as inauthentic and, therefore, ineffective. They develop a style that reflects their distinctive traits and qualities.

STRATEGIES, TIPS & TECHNIQUES TO APPLY

Leaders can't lead without followers. The follower either accepts or rejects the influence of the leader; acceptance is determined by the interaction between the two. All individuals have personal and varying needs, and leaders acquire followers when they are able to assist them in satisfying those needs. If they fail to help their employees in this way, leaders will quickly lose their ability to lead.

There are seven major styles that leaders generally embrace. These styles have a direct effect on organizational performance and results. However, no single definition or style can account for the actions of all leaders. The most effective individuals create a unique method that alternates among the most common styles, or blends multiple approaches seamlessly. The combination or selection of styles can vary according to the demands of a specific situation. Below are the common leadership styles, their uses and characteristics.

The Coercive or Autocratic Style: "Do what I tell you!"

This leadership style is what most people see when they think about "management." Autocratic individuals demand immediate compliance to whatever is dictated. They are often independent and can be seen as a problem for a company because they don't fit in well with their demeaning and bullying nature. The coercive or autocratic leader is considered self-focused and unconcerned with the overall good of the organization.

This leadership style causes the most challenges for organizations. It is difficult to imagine more than one of these leaders within an organization without having substantial social turbulence, chaos and conflict. When used alone, this style is the least effective in any organizational setting. However, it does serve a particular use in certain situations: it can break stubborn negative habits in the workplace and shock employees into accepting new ways of working. With this style, positive long-term results are not created—but internal frustrations and conflict are.

The Authoritative Style: "Come with me and share the experience"

This style is often the most exciting. Leaders who apply it are visionaries. They are capable of creating a cult-like atmosphere within an organization, and they go to great lengths to promote their personal vision of the organization to other associates, employees, customers, suppliers and vendors. This style maximizes commitment to the organization's goals and strategies. Authoritative leaders frame individual tasks and assignments around a great vision with clearly defined standards. These leaders offer effective performance feedback, both positive and negative, that revolves around their plans for the organization.

The design team for the Macintosh computer was extremely successful in applying this style. Its leaders promoted a cult-like culture associated with Macintosh that has endured among its users since its creation in 1984.

The Affiliative or Sympathetic Style: "My people come first above all else"

Affiliative leaders are those who have a great deal of empathy for their employees, and take the time to completely understand them. Leaders applying this style tend to value their employees' emotions more than specific tasks and goals. They have the ability to motivate their employees, as they have taken the time to understand what sparks each of them. These bonds help create happiness and harmony in the organization.

This style positively affects communication, as it leads others to openly share their ideas, inspiring passion and building trust. Flexibility among employees increases with the use of this style because it allows everyone the freedom to do their jobs in the way they feel is most effective.

The Democratic Style: "What do you feel is the best thing to do?"

Activist leaders often utilize this style to challenge the status quo in the organization by questioning existing methods and operations. These leaders build trust, respect and commitment by getting employees to buy in to new ideas that are often generated by others in the organization. This style allows leaders to learn from coworkers. It keeps morale high in spite of any difficult circumstances that might unexpectedly emerge. Democratic leaders give followers a realistic perspective on what they can and cannot accomplish. This approach works effectively when leaders themselves are uncertain about the best direction to take and when they need guidance and direction to get things done more effectively.

Utilizing this style can have its drawbacks. It can lead to endless meetings where ideas are overanalyzed, consensus remains elusive and the only visible results are found in the need to reschedule more meetings. When major decisions need to be made under this style, employees can easily end up confused, causing leadership to subside. This style only works well when employees are completely competent and informed enough to offer effective advice and input.

If leaders successfully apply this style, they can rapidly ascend through the organization. Conversely, they can find their careers quickly limited if things don't go well.

The Pacesetting or Energetic Style: "Let's get moving on it…now!"

This style is typical of energetic leaders. They attract their followers through personal levels of high energy. These leaders are generally "Type A" personalities who are effective at organizing and getting things done. Their personal pace motivates and energizes other individuals, creating synergy. These leaders set extremely high performance standards and serve as personal examples. They actively pinpoint poor performers and demand more from them. If employees fail to rise to the leader's expectations, they get replaced by others who will.

This style also has drawbacks. Generally, the pacesetter either falls short of giving adequate and effective feedback to employees, or jumps in to take over when situations begin to lag. If a pacesetter leaves his or her position, employees suddenly become directionless. As such, this style should be applied sparingly. It works best when all employees have reached the point of being self-motivated and competent enough to need little direction and coordination.

The Coaching Style: "Try this approach"

This style attracts hands-on leaders. They spend a great deal of time with employees on the front lines of the organization where they feel the focal point of the business lies and their time and energy should be devoted. These leaders identify employees' strengths and weaknesses and encourage them to develop and establish long-term goals. They also help individuals conceptualize a plan for attaining their goals. Because of their attitude and personal involvement, these leaders foster a deep sense of employee loyalty.

These leaders primarily emphasize long-term learning for their employees. Even though this style works best, it is often the least used, as many leaders don't have the necessary time for it, especially in high-pressure economic times. It is a slow process and time-consuming task to teach and train employees how to grow and develop effectively.

This style works well when employees are fully aware of their weaknesses and genuinely want to improve their overall performance. However, it becomes ineffective when employees are reluctant to learn and change their behaviors. In order for this style to work to its full potential, leaders must have the expertise to help employees grow and to motivate and analyze situations thoroughly.

The Laissez-Faire Style: "It's up to you"

Leaders who depend on this style exercise little control over their group of employees. It is a dangerous style because it leaves employees to sort out their own roles and tackle their own problems, with little guidance and participation from the leader. It can leave employees directionless.

There are times that this style does work effectively though—for instance, with a high-spirited team of motivated and skilled individuals who have produced proven results in the past. Once these leaders have established that their team is confident, capable and motivated, they step back and let it get on with the task at hand.

Individuals that utilize this style assume that leader interference can generate resentment and detract from the team's effectiveness. Leaders who are willing to hand over control in order to empower their employees to achieve goals, directives and objectives, will apply this style quite consistently.

POINTS TO PONDER — SOMETHING TO THINK ABOUT

1. In the past, what was your personal perception and definition of a leader? Did you define yourself as one?
2. What do you currently believe defines a successful leader?

TRAINING ACTIVITY — APPLICATION & ACTION PLAN

Personal leadership styles tend to be a blend of different elements from various styles. Define your personal leadership style using the list below. If necessary, add additional elements to comprehensively define your unique style.

- Coercive or Autocratic Style
- Authoritative Style
- Affiliative or Sympathetic Style
- Democratic Style
- Pacesetting or Energetic Style
- Coaching Style
- Laissez-Faire Style

Leadership Styles Do Have an Impact

An individual's leadership style is intertwined with his or her particular thought processes, beliefs, experiences and perceptions. Leaders are often unaware of exactly how their leadership style is perceived by others. Nevertheless, these styles, which correspond to a leader's emotional intelligence, do create an impact.

IMPLICATIONS — WHAT THIS MEANS TO YOU

Leadership styles are related to the roles or skills leaders utilize to focus on the organization and its goals and to change employee behavior. A number of studies have indicated a correlation between an individual's leadership style and his or her emotional intelligence. In other words, each leader has a different propensity for applying styles based upon his or her innate personality. However, styles can be learned, and leaders need to utilize several of them to be totally effective. No matter which particular style is developed and nurtured, it will undoubtedly have a tremendous impact on the work climate and employee satisfaction and motivation.

STRATEGIES, TIPS & TECHNIQUES TO APPLY

Effectively using styles to lead is all about achieving results. And the results from applying a particular leadership style are intertwined with the emotional intelligence of an individual leader. Emotional intelligence consists of five dimensions, or capabilities, including:

- Self-awareness
- Self-regulation
- Self-leadership
- Social awareness
- Social skills

The first step toward adopting an effective leadership style is to understand the elements and variables of each dimension.

Self-Awareness

Self-awareness is the ability to understand oneself. Individuals must be aware of their feelings and how those feelings impact them personally, influence their job performance and affect other people.

With self-awareness, individuals can learn to motivate themselves, which is an essential part of successful leadership. Moreover, they can discover a passion for work and a personal desire to achieve. The motivated leader is persistent and highly likely to succeed in attaining his or her goals. The motivated leader is also proactive, initiating tasks and assignments while inspiring his or her employees.

Self-Regulation

Self-regulation is the ability to control oneself and any related emotions. Grasping this dimension involves consciously choosing an appropriate emotional response when interacting with people and events. Also, when necessary, it involves channeling emotions in productive ways. Self-regulation eliminates the wasted time and energy of negative emotional responses that can cripple an organization.

Leaders who have high levels of self-regulation foster a climate of trust and fairness, and attract talented individuals to their teams. They also focus on issues rather than personal agendas and internal politics.

Self-Leadership

Self-leadership is the ability to manage oneself. This dimension is important because research has shown that many leaders have problems in three related areas:

- Difficulty handling change
- Inability to work within a team
- Poor interpersonal relationships

Often leaders have a tendency to focus on their needs rather than those of their employees. Without the capacity to expand their perspectives and understand their employees' points of view, these leaders lack the flexibility to change, have difficulty collaborating with teams and cannot relate well to others, even when they have the opportunity to effect results.

Social Awareness

Social awareness is the ability to understand others through empathy. Empathy entails seeing things from another person's perspective. Leaders with strong empathy skills can understand not only what the other person is saying, but also where the person's feelings may come from.

While empathy allows leaders to understand others, it starts when they understand their own feelings. This quality is a critical component in effective communication and leadership. Conversely, a lack of empathy is the primary cause of interpersonal problems, as well as issues with customers, vendors and suppliers.

Social Skills

Social skills allow leaders to actually lead others. This dimension brings the other four together, allowing the leader to apply them in the following ways:

- Understand others, sense their feelings and perspectives, and take an active interest in their concerns.
- Develop a service orientation to anticipate, recognize and meet customer needs.

- Cultivate opportunities by bringing together a diversity of people, perspectives and viewpoints.
- Interpret the political and social climate and any other currents in the organization.

POINTS TO PONDER — SOMETHING TO THINK ABOUT

1. In terms of self-awareness, self-regulation, self-leadership, social awareness and social skills, where do you feel your greatest strength lies? Why?
2. How do you think others interpret your leadership characteristics and style?

TRAINING ACTIVITY — APPLICATION & ACTION PLAN

In each of the areas below, identify how your thought processes, beliefs, experiences and perceptions have an impact. Develop a chart outlining your strengths and weaknesses in order to identify elements that need improvement.

- Self-awareness
- Self-regulation
- Self-leadership
- Social awareness
- Social skills

What Is the Best Leadership Style?

Research indicates that leaders showing the best results do not rely on a single leadership style; rather, they have the ability to switch seamlessly into one that best fits the particular situation. They can intuitively sense the challenge and apply the appropriate leadership style to meet it.

IMPLICATIONS — WHAT THIS MEANS TO YOU

Studies also show that the more styles a leader utilizes, the better. The most effective leaders are sensitive to situations and are able to adjust their personal styles to obtain the best results. These leaders acquire a natural habit to change styles as needed.

It is important for leaders to understand that there is not just one definitive and typical leadership style. The aforementioned studies indicate that leaders who master four or more styles—especially the varieties known as authoritative, democratic, affiliative and coaching—foster the best work climate and demonstrate the greatest increases in workplace and organizational performance.

STRATEGIES, TIPS & TECHNIQUES TO APPLY

Before leaders can assess the most effective style(s) for themselves, they must understand the impact of each in relation to the organizational climate. There are six factors that influence an organization's working environment:

- **Flexibility** – To what degree are employees free to be innovative without bureaucratic interference?
- **Responsibility** – Employees feel a sense of duty toward their organization.
- **Standards** – Individuals set performance standards for themselves and expect accurate feedback.
- **Rewards** – How apt are rewards for personal performance?
- **Clarity** – How well do employees understand the mission and values of the organization?
- **Commitment** – What is the level of commitment to a common goal or purpose?

All leadership styles have a measurable impact on each aspect of the organizational climate. The effectiveness of each style can be evaluated in various situations, and results are based upon its subsequent effect on the above factors. Extensive research shows that leaders who use styles that positively impact the organizational climate create financial results superior to those leaders who impact the organizational climate negatively. Discussed below are predominate leadership styles along with the strengths and weaknesses of each.

The Coercive Style

The coercive style demands immediate compliance from employees, generally making it the least effective style in the workplace. The consistent use of this style completely destroys a subordinate's sense of personal motivation. Most employees are motivated by more than money: they seek satisfaction in the pride of doing a good job. The coercive style often obliterates personal satisfaction because it quashes innovation and flexibility, and shatters any sense of empowerment employees feel. In fact, this style is so harsh many employees develop a personal resentment toward most leaders who use it, and they begin to rebel if it is used all the time. Once this style oppresses employees long enough, they will do everything and anything to undermine the leader's authority.

While the coercive style spawns compliance and actions that are almost exclusively derived from fear (therefore extremely short-lived), it can occasionally produce results.

There are two unique situations where this style is perhaps effective and appropriate to apply: first, when an emergency has occurred within the organization and someone needs to take charge quickly and be in absolute control; second, when an employee needs a call to action and must be shocked into breaking old habits. In both instances this style should be used carefully and in a limited manner.

The Authoritative Style

The authoritative style mobilizes employees toward a common vision. Authoritative leaders are known for both their enthusiasm and clear vision. Their effectiveness rests on their ability to motivate employees by showing each one how his or her work fits into the bigger picture of the company and correlates with overall organizational results. Utilizing these connections, authoritative leaders have the ability to define specific standards that support their vision. Because leaders define goals, objectives, strategies, expectations, assignments and results through their vision, they make certain to provide their employees with the flexibility to innovate, experiment and take risks to accomplish their defined tasks, projects and responsibilities.

The authoritative leadership style is appropriate for nearly any organizational situation. However, it does not work well when a leader is collaborating with more experienced or seasoned individuals.

The Affiliative Style

The affiliative leader fosters harmony among employees and builds emotional bonds. Consequently, this leader creates a workforce that is intensely loyal to him or her. This style greatly enhances communication and positive feedback. The bonds that are created intensify organizational cohesiveness, flexibility and trust among employees. Because of these factors, employees feel a strong sense of belonging, caring and responsibility in relation to both the leader and the organization.

The affiliative leadership style is effective and should be utilized when leaders are attempting to build and foster team harmony, increase morale, improve communication and, when the need arises, reestablish broken trust. When this particular style is linked with the authoritative style it creates a powerful combination for any leader to employ.

The Democratic Style

The democratic style allows leaders to invest time to solicit employees' ideas, insights and feedback. As a result, this leader builds trust, respect and commitment. By allowing employees to have a say in the decisions that affect them, the leader increases both flexibility and responsibility. Additionally, employees working with a democratic leader have the tendency to be more realistic about what they can achieve and accomplish.

One downside of employing this style is that the team can develop a propensity to rely on a seemingly endless number of meetings in order to arrive at a general consensus. Furthermore, employees may end up confused and leaderless in certain situations.

This style works best when a leader is uncertain about the best direction to take, and desires insight and feedback from employees. It also works well for generating fresh ideas and perspectives within the organization.

The Pacesetting Style

Pacesetting leaders develop a high performance situation for themselves and their employees. The same level of excellence is required of both. If the employee cannot produce, he or she is quickly replaced. Conscientiousness, a personal drive to achieve, and high levels of initiative identify pacesetting leaders. This style is appropriate for directing and overseeing a competent and motivated team of employees who need little or no direction. In most other instances, this style destroys the organizational climate. Morale can plummet as employees find it difficult to keep pace with or anticipate the demands of the leader. It is recommended that this leadership style be blended with another one in order to make it more effective.

The Coaching Style

The coaching style of leadership focuses on developing employees for the future. These leaders help their employees identify key strengths and weaknesses and then link them to their long-term career goals. Leaders using this style are more like mentors and counselors than traditional superiors: they are excellent at delegating tasks and assigning challenging assignments. While most leaders feel too pressured to use this style, it can have a dramatic impact on the organizational climate and the overall performance of employees.

POINTS TO PONDER — SOMETHING TO THINK ABOUT

1. Which leadership styles do you think you incorporate when you feel comfortable as a leader?
2. Can you identify a particular time where you may have applied an inappropriate leadership style to a specific situation?

TRAINING ACTIVITY — APPLICATION & ACTION PLAN

Identify six specific situations where each of the following, or a combination of the six leadership styles, would apply.

- Coercive
- Authoritative
- Affiliative
- Democratic
- Pacesetting
- Coaching

Gauging the Pitfalls of Leadership Styles

here is a time and place for applying each of the six leadership styles. Potential failures occur with the misapplication of a style, a particularly unsuitable combination of styles, or the failure to understand the pitfalls related to each.

IMPLICATIONS — WHAT THIS MEANS TO YOU

A leader should keep an arsenal of leadership styles at his or her disposal. Each has specific applications and purposes to advance the organization. While the application of one style can have a positive impact on a situation, a different style applied to the exact same set of circumstances can have a negative outcome.

Words and actions do in fact have meanings that create specific perceptions in employees' minds. That is why the application of an inappropriate leadership style can communicate the wrong message and have severe ramifications and complications for the organization.

STRATEGIES, TIPS & TECHNIQUES TO APPLY

The most common pitfall most leaders encounter is applying the wrong leadership style to a specific situation. For example, a leader may have to inform his or her employees of problems within the organization that could ultimately result in layoffs. This is a potentially explosive situation that has clear ramifications on morale and the retention of key employees. When dealing with this situation, different leadership styles can have vastly different outcomes.

In one case, a coercive leader can take charge and deal with the situation. This leader will take a no-nonsense approach that can frighten employees and completely demoralize them. Rather than deal sensitively with employee emotions, the coercive leader discounts such feelings and ultimately provokes key employees into quitting, damaging the organization further.

The ideal approach would be to use the affiliative and democratic styles together. The democratic style allows employees to get involved in the process, voice their concerns, and provide feedback and insight regarding possible solutions. The combination of the democratic and affiliative styles allows the leader to empathize with his or her employees, heal any rifts within the organization and facilitate open communication. This marriage of the two also allows employees to explore options and arrive at mutually agreeable conclusions. While these positive ends may be achieved with any leadership style, the proper approach reduces any further damage while developing potentially new options to arrive at an amicable solution.

It should be noted that there are specific pitfalls associated with all leadership styles, which leaders should be aware of. The pitfalls pertaining to each style are discussed below.

The Coercive Style

The coercive leadership style has an overall negative impact on the organizational climate. It should be used sparingly, only when circumstances truly warrant it. Leaders that continually use this style will find it can ruin the organizational climate because of the leader's insensitivity to the morale and feelings of employees under his or her direction.

The Authoritative Style

While the authoritative leadership style is generally a good style to apply, it fails when a leader works with a team of experts or individuals more experienced that he or she is. In these instances the leader may appear to be pompous or out of touch.

In other instances, if a leader becomes too overbearing when using this style, the cooperative spirit of the organization can be undermined.

The Affiliative Style

The affiliative leadership style's exclusive focus on praising employee performance can cause underperformance to go uncorrected. In these instances, lagging employees may perceive that their standard of performance is tolerated.

Furthermore, since affiliative leaders tend to focus on giving praise rather than dispensing specific advice and directives on how to handle challenging tasks and assignments, employees may feel that they are not receiving sufficient guidance. Such lack of direction can lead to employee confusion and poor performance. If used exclusively, this style can also lead to organizational failure.

The Democratic Style

While the democratic style is effective in building consensus, the process can get bogged down in endless meetings. In the end, employees can feel confused and leaderless. Additionally, this style is clearly ineffective when employees are not competent or informed enough to offer sound advice and realistic feedback. It also fails during company crises and emergencies, where applying a democratic style will only result in creating total chaos.

The Pacesetting Style

The pacesetting leadership style is capable of destroying the entire organizational climate. Employees may feel overwhelmed by the high standards a pacesetting leader expects of them. Those who use this style may often know what they want and expect, but fail to clearly communicate these desires to their employees. Consequently, employees begin to second-guess the leader while attempting to anticipate his or her demands.

Also, because of this leader's impatience, employees feel he or she doesn't trust them enough to take initiative or have a deep enough belief in their capabilities to allow them the flexibility to innovate. Consequently, morale and commitment are greatly diminished, as employees don't understand how their contributions fit into the overall organizational plan.

The Coaching Style

The coaching style works best with employees who see the benefits of being coached; it is ineffective with employees who are resistant to learning or change. The coaching style fails when leaders lack the expertise to help an employee overcome particular job-related weaknesses, issues or concerns. Applying this style while lacking professional expertise instills fear and apathy in employees, when, instead, they require the leader to motivate them with ongoing performance feedback.

POINTS TO PONDER — SOMETHING TO THINK ABOUT

1. Can you identify a situation where an inappropriate style should have been replaced with a style better suited to handle the problem? Do you feel the results would have changed? How?
2. Are you aware of how your leadership style directly affects your employees, their morale and their performance?

TRAINING ACTIVITY — APPLICATION & ACTION PLAN

Identify a specific problem or situation you have encountered. Take this scenario and apply each of the six leadership styles to it. Further develop the scenario to identify possible employee reactions and the ultimate results for each.

- Coercive
- Authoritative

- Affiliative
- Democratic
- Pacesetting
- Coaching

Keys to Developing an Effective Leadership Style

Effective management requires a fostering of positive moods and actions throughout the organization. This can only be accomplished after leaders apply a reflective analysis of their personal behaviors and the subsequent impacts. Studies continually show that there is a clear correlation between a leader's behavior and the performance outcomes of an organization. In essence, a leader's mood and behavior set the tone for the entire organization.

IMPLICATIONS — WHAT THIS MEANS TO YOU

To positively impact moods and behaviors in an organization, leaders are required to go beyond simply donning a façade of serious and motivated commitment to the job: they must display genuine and sincere moods and behaviors on a consistent basis. Research consistently indicates that a leader's emotional intelligence, demonstrated through his or her moods and behaviors, is readily communicated throughout an entire organization. A leader's mood is contagious and spreads quickly and inexorably.

Leaders need to ensure that they regularly display an authentic, optimistic and high-energy mood. Additionally, they must make sure their employees feel and act in a similar fashion. Leaders must understand the impact that their moods have upon their organization and take care to effectively manage them. Research clearly demonstrates a connection between a leader's mood and the organization's bottom-line performance.

STRATEGIES, TIPS & TECHNIQUES TO APPLY

The aforementioned studies have consistently demonstrated that effective leaders display personal moods and behaviors that match the circumstances and situations they are in, mixed with a healthy dose of optimism. These leaders show respect for how other individuals feel at any particular moment while modeling specific behavior traits that display an optimistic future. This type of management is called "resonant behavior," and it utilizes all of the elements of emotional intelligence, which are discussed below.

Self-Awareness

Self-awareness is the ability of leaders to understand and comprehend their own emotions. Self-awareness is closely aligned with a sense of self-worth because it allows individuals to know their personal strengths and weaknesses. With this knowledge they are confident in grasping their own personal value. Resonant leaders use self-awareness to accurately gauge and interpret their personal moods and to analyze and determine how each one affects others within the organization.

Self-Management

Self-management is the ability of leaders to control their emotions. When leaders competently manage their personal emotions, they are able to act with honesty and integrity in a manner that allows them to adapt themselves to varied circumstances. While everyone has an occasional bad day, resonant leaders use self-management techniques to help keep their bad moods from tainting the workplace. They can explain the situational causes for their bad mood so others know where it is coming from, and can figure its expected duration.

Social Awareness

Socially aware leaders not only sense other individuals' emotions but also sincerely demonstrate a genuine care for their people. The key elements of social awareness are empathy and organizational intuition. Resonant leaders are extremely aware of how their words and actions directly affect and impact others. They are sensitive and can deeply reflect upon and analyze other peoples' moods, emotions and feelings. If these leaders feel their words and behaviors could result in producing negative consequences, they intuitively buffer their communication and actions to minimize the impact.

Relationship Management

Relationship management includes applying management skills that communicate clearly and methods that are effective in disarming conflicts. These skills and methods give leaders the ability to create strong and enduring bonds with others. Resonant leaders use these qualities to passionately communicate their enthusiasm and to resolve conflicts with both humor and kindness. While this is an effective mode of leadership, it is the one most rarely demonstrated; individuals more often experience the toxic moods of dissonant superiors whose behaviors create chaos and havoc in an organization.

POINTS TO PONDER — SOMETHING TO THINK ABOUT

1. How observant have you been about the impact of your personal moods and behaviors upon others in your department and organization?
2. Can you cite a circumstance where your mood or behavior (negative or positive) had a significant impact on your employees?

TRAINING ACTIVITY — APPLICATION & ACTION PLAN

Create a diary or log of your personal moods and behaviors. As you document your daily mood swings, assess and gauge the impact they have on your employees and workplace. The four emotional intelligence elements should be observed and noted.

- Self-awareness
- Self-management
- Social awareness
- Relationship management

Losing Your Leadership Style Can Undermine Your Performance

Numerous studies have shown that when leaders are in a happy mood, the individuals around them tend to view everything in a much more positive light. The resulting atmosphere provides for an optimistic workplace, which in turn facilitates higher overall productivity, more creative reasoning and more efficient decision making. The converse is often true when a leader's negative moods prevail: they have detrimental effects for the leader, his or her employees and the organization's performance.

IMPLICATIONS — WHAT THIS MEANS TO YOU

In 2000, Caroline Bartel of New York University and Richard Saavedra of the University of Michigan studied 70 workgroups across diverse industries. Their research found that people who gather within normal meeting settings end up sharing their good or bad moods within two hours. Other research has corroborated the fact that people who work together share their moods.

It is significant for leaders to understand that within most organizations, moods that originate at the top have a tendency to spread quickly throughout the workplace. The reason for this diffusion is that nearly everyone in the company observes these moods and is thus directly influenced by them. Leader's that are not cognizant of this process fail to understand the personal impact they, and their moods, have on organizational performance.

STRATEGIES, TIPS & TECHNIQUES TO APPLY

A large body of research indicates that a majority of leaders are unaware that their emotional intelligence levels, their moods and their behaviors have a definite impact on employees and the organization. Leaders can remain clueless as to how these factors have the power to resonate throughout an organization. In many instances the repercussions of unwatched and uncontrolled negative behaviors are immediate. Employees can be reluctant to communicate accurate and realistic data and information for fear of the leader's emotional reaction and potential rage.

The consequences of negative emotional reactions are damaging to the point that the leader becomes emotionally disconnected from the organization; as a result, he or she will not have a realistic sense of what is occurring in the workplace. These circumstances are especially troubling when employees actively work to hide failures, mistakes and potentially troubling trends. While an emotionally disconnected leader can often sense something is amiss in the workplace, the exact cause remains elusive and their personal effectiveness is thus undermined. The perceived uncertainty of the situation also forces leaders to second-guess their employees. Other serious organizational problems can be caused by the following reasons:

Lack of Awareness

When leaders demonstrate a lack of personal awareness, they cannot objectively gauge their own personal moods let alone the impact those moods have on the organization. In some instances, a lack of awareness is the result of the leader's ignorance, but more often it is a reflection of older leadership styles being used.

Many leaders who fall victim to a lack of awareness feel their personal moods are nobody's business. Because these leaders do not see the need to force themselves to accommodate their employees, it becomes their employees' responsibility to deal with the moods. Whatever the cause and reason, a lack of personal awareness undermines not only the leader's effectiveness, but also the bottom-line performance of their organization.

Lack of Self-Management

When leaders possess a lack of self-management skills, it can be toxic to an organization. Mood swings, highly emotional responses, rages and outbursts have a dramatic and negative impact on all employees. In all these instances, leaders allow their emotions to control them. These uncontrolled emotions serve to undermine employee motivation and morale, which produces immediate and negative consequences on organizational productivity.

When leaders allow themselves to be emotionally unstable, their organization will experience higher rates of absenteeism and employee turnover due to increased stress levels. This tangible impact on an organization can be directly analyzed, quantified and demonstrated.

Lack of Social Awareness

Leaders clearly lack social awareness when they fail to empathize with employees and other individuals. Those who lack social awareness are either unaware a problem in this area exists or they don't care about the impact their words and actions have on employees and the organization. Leaders who only focus on results while neglecting personal contributions, actively demonstrate this social deficiency.

Such leaders are unconcerned about motivation, morale or personal issues. Consequently, they will often find themselves surrounded by incompetent or fearful employees. The competent individuals or those with better employment options will quickly leave. The subsequent impact on the company's productivity and profitability will be serious and obvious.

Poor Relationship Management

Leaders who possess poor relationship management skills are unable to communicate effectively, which results in misunderstandings, confusion and conflict. Employees in this situation can feel leaderless and uncommitted, as their work is often criticized and second-guessed by the leader. The leader's poor relationships with employees subsequently lower morale and motivation. Employees don't know where they stand with these leaders. And this feeling often results in high employee turnover and lower productivity.

While possible, it is uncommon for leaders to exhibit symptoms in only one of the above areas: usually they are deficient in multiple emotional intelligence categories. When these factors are combined, their impacts are intensified; a toxic organizational atmosphere is thus created that is saturated with problems and conflicts. Often these leaders cause extreme chaos and havoc within the entire organization. Not only does this diminish *their* standing and effectiveness as a leader, but also it can completely undermine and destroy an *organization's* effectiveness. Turmoil and damage will remain until a more hopeful and realistic leader replaces the dissonant one. And this change generally becomes the only viable alternative to relieve chaos and repair the organization.

POINTS TO PONDER — SOMETHING TO THINK ABOUT

1. Have you ever worked under the direction of a moody or emotional individual? If yes, how did you feel about your work?
2. Conversely, have you ever worked under the direction of an optimistic and motivational individual? How did you feel about your work and responsibilities under his or her direction?

TRAINING ACTIVITY — APPLICATION & ACTION PLAN

1. Write a set of employee workplace instructions.
2. Consider and evaluate from a positive and a negative viewpoint the potential impact these instructions may have on your employees.
3. Take time to rewrite the instructions from several perspectives.
4. Compare and contrast the various impacts.

What Constitutes the Empowered Leader?

Leaders lead and managers manage. There is a definite difference between the two: managers direct while leaders motivate and inspire their employees. In the business world there are managers who are not leaders and leaders who are not managers. Ideally, managers should be leaders, capable of motivating, empowering, securely guiding, and supporting their team to reach greater heights of achievement in whatever task is assigned to them.

IMPLICATIONS — WHAT THIS MEANS TO YOU

An empowered leader is determined by specific characteristics and criteria. The primary goal is to build a highly effective workplace within the organization; the leader's actions must be consistent to support that end. Positive leadership behavior is the differentiating factor that makes someone highly effective and indispensable to his or her staff and company.

The principles and actions of empowered leadership put the leader's focus directly on the needs of their team of subordinates to facilitate the accomplishment of specific goals. By focusing on personal empowerment through delegation, leaders can foster outstanding team performance.

STRATEGIES, TIPS & TECHNIQUES TO APPLY

Empowered leaders are attuned to the expectations their employees have of them; traditional managers, on the other hand, tend to focus on the specifics of attaining goals and objectives to increase productivity. A leader's actions are always directed toward four expectations of their employees: that they build security, practice fairness and justice, focus upon individual fulfillment, and create a sense of personal involvement.

Empowered leaders continually work to create strong, efficient, highly effective workforces that operate in an environment of trust, respect and acceptance. In order to achieve these specific goals, leaders can utilize the principles and actions discussed below.

Move Away from Control and into Empowerment

Effective leaders always apply the principles of empowerment to create a positive workplace environment where the feelings of others are taken into consideration. Many traditional managers, however, have difficulty relinquishing control. This is understandable since a manager's position often requires strict responsibility and accountability for the results of his or her department.

Before employees are able to embrace the idea of leadership in their workplace, managerial control must evolve into empowerment, motivation and delegation. The outcome of this shift builds a sense of workforce security, involvement and fulfillment that in turn produces increased tangible results. To enact a workable empowerment strategy, leaders must embrace the following guidelines:

- Replace managerial control with actions that emphasize all individual input will be taken seriously and given respectful consideration. Managers often like to play it safe rather than take a risk; however, empowered leaders understand that risk comes with increased opportunity.
- Ask for and accept input, assuring employees that it will be acted upon and that credit will be given where it is due. This technique improves motivation and performance because trust and loyalty are emphasized. Skillfully using delegation and cooperation helps build workplace strength, values and ethics.

- Create a sense of workplace ownership in everything accomplished. Managers often prefer to stifle creativity in the workplace because they don't want to disrupt the balance; empowered leaders understand that change and progress must come with some risk attached.

Use Motivation to Replace Orders

When it comes to maintaining workforce effectiveness and structure, managers often confuse motivation with the vocal assertions of "cannot," "will not" and "do not." In fact, positive motivation focuses on sustaining four primary areas in the workplace: security, fairness and justice, personal fulfillment and individual involvement.

When leaders want to increase workforce performance, commanding and dictating do not produce the same results as motivating individuals. Empowered leaders can take several steps to effectively motivate their employees.

- Learn everything possible about the personalities of employees.
- Apply specific motivational techniques with each individual—not general techniques for all.
- Establish a definite relationship between motivation and personal enhancement.
- Apply motivational techniques consistently.
- Demonstrate the motivational factors of cooperation, determination and persistence along with the feeling of success in daily personal actions. Leaders use their own actions to reinforce and display personal motivation.

Remove Self-Sufficiency and Replace It with Cooperation

Many managers find it difficult to delegate due to the pressures of time, the lack of effective individuals to delegate to, and the presumption that they alone are in the position to know how to get something accomplished in the most effective and competent manner.

Effective leaders, on the other hand, take the following actions to produce a greater cooperative effort and build commitment into the workplace atmosphere:

- Know the right individuals to delegate to. Better cooperation comes with identifying and matching the right abilities and talents to the specific tasks needing delegation. Take the time to discuss expectations, timelines, objectives and support.
- Demonstrate that cooperative efforts create a sense of ownership in projects, and share the responsibility for their outcomes.
- Maintain open lines of communication. Produce a cooperative spirit by seriously accepting employee input.
- Openly share daily successes, even if a success seems small. Encouraging and supporting even minor successes creates a unifying atmosphere of care and cooperation.

POINTS TO PONDER — SOMETHING TO THINK ABOUT

1. How have daily time constraints interfered with your empowered leadership focus? What results do you experience?
2. Have you developed any specific leadership goals as part of your daily activities?

TRAINING ACTIVITY — APPLICATION & ACTION PLAN

On a piece of paper create four columns. Label each column as follows: Security; Fairness and Justice; Personal Fulfillment; Personal Involvement.

1. Under each column list four specific techniques you can focus upon.
2. Next to the techniques, list one action you can apply to build increased cooperative efforts for fostering trust and loyalty in your workforce.
3. Apply these actions consistently.
4. List any positive changes you subsequently observe that move you further toward becoming a totally empowered leader.

The Tangible Impact of Leadership Styles on Results

The leadership style and mood of the individual leader does have an impact on the performance and results of the organization. A change in leadership or the application of different leadership styles can cause dramatic shifts in organizational performance—in a positive or negative direction.

IMPLICATIONS — WHAT THIS MEANS TO YOU

It may seem weak or naïvely emotional to many leaders to have a discussion of leadership styles and how each impacts the feelings and morale of individual employees. However, research has clearly demonstrated the significant impact that leadership styles have on the workplace climate.

It is important for leaders to understand that while they may have a predominant leadership style, the most effective leaders use particular styles for specific situations in much the same way that a golfer deliberately selects the best club for making a particular play on the golf course. The key is knowing where and when to use a specific leadership style for maximum effectiveness.

STRATEGIES, TIPS & TECHNIQUES TO APPLY

Research has shown a clear correlation between leadership style selection and financial results such as return on sales, revenue growth, efficiency and profitability. This connection is understandable, as a leader's personal style sets the tone for the workplace climate, which in turn has an effect on results.

Leadership Styles with a Positive Impact

The following styles show beneficial tangible results. They are listed in descending order of impact.

Authoritative – This style has the strongest positive impact on the workplace climate. It produces benefits in the areas of rewards, clarity and standards. There is also a correlation between the use of this style and an increase in flexibility and commitment. However, it lacks somewhat in fostering employee responsibility.

All results combined, this style has a propensity to positively reward employees based upon their performance. Additionally, employees working under this style have a clear understanding of their mission and values, which creates a high standard of performance. They are free to innovate and are committed to a common purpose as set by their leader. The overall effect is positive motivation that produces positive results.

Affiliative – The strengths of this style are similar to the authoritative style, but the overall impact on fostering a positive workplace climate is not as prominent. The major benefit of this style is the high degree of positive feedback affiliative leaders provide to employees, which creates a strong sense of belonging to a cohesive organization. This approach tends to be taken by individuals who are natural relationship builders. The employee motivation created with the use of this style is based on a sense of loyalty to the leader combined with a commitment to follow his or her direction.

Democratic – There is a strong correlation between the use of this style and a positive workplace climate in terms of flexibility, rewards, clarity and commitment. Democratic leaders invest time and effort in gathering feedback and obtaining the allegiance of individual employees, which builds trust, respect and commitment. This style recognizes the individual's personal contribution to the success of the organization while giving employees the opportunity to set their own goals and objectives. A personal sense of empowerment and commitment is fostered because of each person's contributions. It can create a synergistic environment where experimentation and innovation are encouraged, thus sparking new ideas and insights. Because of the latitude employees are given under this style, they are motivated to attain results and the goals they have established for themselves.

Coaching – The use of this style produces a positive workplace climate in terms of rewards, clarity and commitment. The impact should not be minimized because the coaching style requires constant dialogue—and dialogue energizes every driver of workplace climate. The one drawback of this style is that leaders typically feel they do not have the available time to help individual employees grow, as it tends to be a slow and tedious process. However, for the leader who does invest the time, the impacts on workplace climate and performance are markedly positive.

Leadership Styles with a Negative Impact

The following styles have a negative impact on tangible results. They are listed in descending order of impact.

Coercive – There is a strongly harmful correlation between the use of this style and the resulting workplace climate. The only slightly positive outcome is in personal standards. The coercive style influences virtually all aspects of workplace climate, as it destroys personal motivation. Additionally, coercive leadership erodes personal pride and empowerment, and destroys most of the satisfaction that employees derive from a job well done. All of these factors create a drag on performance and undermine productivity. When used for prolonged periods of time, coercive leadership tends to alienate employees. The long-term impact of the leader's insensitivity is disastrous for workplace morale and individual feelings.

Pacesetting – There is a harmful correlation between the use of this style and the resulting workplace environment in the areas of standards, rewards, clarity and commitment. Because leaders employing this style set extremely high-performance standards and expect the same of their employees, many individuals feel overwhelmed. As such, morale and motivation are undermined. Moreover, pacesetting leaders often fail to clearly communicate their standards and expectations, resulting in employee confusion. Since pacesetters create the perception that they don't trust the employee to take the initiative to do his or her job properly, personal motivation and empowerment erode. The overall impact will be seen in declining performance and productivity.

POINTS TO PONDER — SOMETHING TO THINK ABOUT

1. Have you observed the different leadership styles within your own organization and how they have impacted performance?
2. Do you understand how your personal leadership style can impact departmental and organizational performance and results?

TRAINING ACTIVITY — APPLICATION & ACTION PLAN

Identify your predominant leadership style.

1. Assess the impact it has on your organization.
2. Determine how alternative leadership styles might have a more positive influence on performance and results.

About the Author

Timothy F. Bednarz, Ph.D. is CEO of the American Management Development Group, Inc. For over 20 years he has researched, designed and authored hundreds of learning and development programs used by Fortune 1000 companies.

He is also the author of *Great! What Makes Leaders Great. What They Did, How They Did It and What You Can Learn from It* (2011).

Speaking Availability

Timothy F. Bednarz, Ph.D. is available for speaking engagements for your next meeting or association event. He can be contacted at 800-654-4935 or by e-mail at timothy.bednarz@majorium.com.

Bulk Sales

Bulk sales of this book or any other titles available from Majorium Business Press. Inquiries can be directed to sales@majorium.com, or by phone at 800-6654-4935.

Quick Order Form

Fax orders: 715-342-1118. Send this form.

Telephone orders: Call 800-654-4935 toll-free. Have your credit card ready.

Email orders: sales@majorium.com

Postal orders: Majorium Business Press, 2025 Main Street, Stevens Point, WI 54481, USA.

Please send the following books:

____

____

____

____

Please send more FREE information on:

❑Catalog ❑Speaking/Seminars ❑Mailing Lists ❑Consulting

Name: ____

Address: ____

City: ______________________ State: ____ Zip: _______

Telephone: ______________________________________

Email address: ___________________________________

Sales tax: Please add 5.5% for products shipped to Wisconsin addresses.

Shipping by air:

United States: $4.00 for first book and $2.00 for each additional product.

International: $9.00 for first book; $5.00 for each additional product (estimate).

Made in United States
Cleveland, OH
05 November 2026

47664312R00030